My Filipino Word Book

English - Tagálog - Ilokáno

Robin Lyn Fancy and Vala Jeanne Welch
Illustrated by Ronny Lynn
Edited by Imelda Fines Gasmen

3565 Harding Avenue
Honolulu, Hawai'i 96816
toll free: (800) 910-2377
phone: (808) 734-7159
fax: (808) 732-3627
e-mail: sales@besspress.com
www.besspress.com

Design: Carol Colbath

Cataloging-in-publication data

Fancy, Robin Lyn.
  My Filipino word book / Robin Lyn
  Fancy and Vala Jeanne Welch ;
  editor : Imelda Fines Gasmen.
         p.   cm.
  Includes illustrations.
  ISBN 13: 978-1-57306-276-3
  1. Philippine languages—Glossaries,
vocabularies, etc. 2. Tagalog
language—Glossaries, vocabularies, etc.
3. Iloko language—Glossaries, vocabularies,
etc. I. Welch, Vala Jeanne. II. Gasmen,
Imelda Fines. III. Title.
PL5506.F36 2007   499.21-dc21

Printed in China

Contents

Acknowledgments

We would like to gratefully acknowledge a grant from the Robert E. Black Fund of the Hawaii Community Foundation. We are also grateful to Kunpang Lana'i—Coalition For a Drug Free Lana'i for supporting this literacy project for Filipino youth.

Robin Lyn Fancy is the school librarian and Vala Jeanne Welch teaches at Lāna'i High and Elementary.

English	red
Tagálog	pulá
Ilokáno	nalabága

English	orange
Tagálog	órens; kúlay-dalandán
Ilokáno	órens; narángha

English	yellow
Tagálog	diláw
Ilokáno	amarílio

English	green
Tagálog	bérde
Ilokáno	bérde

English	blue
Tagálog	asúl; bugháw
Ilokáno	asúl

English	violet
Tagálog	kúlay-úbe; lila
Ilokáno	kolór ti úbe

English	square
Tagálog	kuwadrádo; parisukát
Ilokáno	kuadrádo

English	rectangle
Tagálog	rektángguló; parihabá
Ilokáno	rektánggulo

English   triangle

Tagálog   triyánggulo; tatsulók

Ilokáno   trayánggulo

English   circle

Tagálog   bilóg

Ilokáno   nagbukél

English   star

Tagálog   húgis-bituwín

Ilokáno   sinán-bituén

English	heart
Tagálog	húgis-púsó
Ilokáno	sinán-púso

English   one

Tagálog   isá

Ilokáno   maysá

English	two
Tagálog	dalawá
Ilokáno	duá

English	three
Tagálog	tatló
Ilokáno	talló

English   four

Tagálog   ápat

Ilokáno   uppát

English five

Tagálog limá

Ilokáno limá

English   six

Tagálog   ánim

Ilokáno   inném

English	seven
Tagálog	**pitó**
Ilokáno	**pitó**

English	eight
Tagálog	waló
Ilokáno	waló

English	nine
Tagálog	siyám
Ilokáno	siám

English	ten
Tagálog	sampú
Ilokáno	sangapúlo

English	cat
Tagálog	púsá
Ilokáno	púsa

English	dog
Tagálog	áso
Ilokáno	áso

English	rooster
Tagálog	tandáng
Ilokáno	kawítan

English   goat

Tagálog   kambíng

Ilokáno   kaldíng

English	carabao
Tagálog	kalabáw
Ilokáno	nuwáng

English	bird
Tagálog	íbon
Ilokáno	billít